Disha Prabha

Guided Light for Spiritual Seekers

SHARANYA DINESH

AuthorHouse™ UK
1663 Liberty Drive
Bloomington, IN 47403 USA
www.authorhouse.co.uk
Phone: 0800.197.4150

Published by AuthorHouse 12/17/2018

ISBN: 978-1-5462-9835-9 (sc)
ISBN: 978-1-5462-9834-2 (e)

authorHOUSE®

Author's Note:

Master used to say: "All knowledge comes by doing something and then writing about it ..."

Dear All,

'Disha Prabha' is the connecting link of this series, and has a special significance too. Thus, I commence this series with the etymology of the name. When we (the lazy intellectual better half that I am married to and the earnest me) were searching for an ideal name for my counseling practice, we tried various permutations and combinations; for a word, phrase which meant 'to throw light on' or 'to guide' or 'give direction' because as a counselor that was my ideal job description. The other thought which we were consciously coming back to was, a name that would have the family members in it (the four of us), so that one name would suffice as our 'house sign board' and my 'practice title'.

Thus, Disha Prabha came into being. Disha means direction or way, and Praha means illumination or radiance. This was just perfect; counselling is all about 'Lighting the Way' or lending 'radiance to direction' and more importantly -

Disha is a combination of Di - Dinesh (the boss of the family) and Sha - Sharanya (the author) and Prabha is put together with Pra - Pranav (our son) and Bha - Bhargavi (our daughter). So, in unanimous consensus we chose this name.

Most of my writings are experiences or moments shared with these three people. It is but obvious that they make an appearance everywhere, in this book and all the other books that will follow.

This book is the first of Disha Prabha series. And a 'thank you' to 'Sahaj Marg' (the meditation path I follow and teach) ; my Disha received Prabha from this Path and I owe everything to this Path.

Now, a bit about me,

I am a Behavioral Counselor and a Psychotherapist as far as academics is concerned. But inherently I am a seeker, trying to learn something new every day and trying to improve myself with every learning that I receive. Not just live, but be alive and continue to live even after death catches up on me someday. This spirit of enquiry has led me to dabble with many vocations like music, sketching, Painting, cooking and writing (verily a dilettante). I am an instinctive writer and enjoy sharing my experiences and learnings; and this book and the ones that will follow are a compilation of such experiences and learnings.

I have a keen interest in bringing self-awareness amongst children; help them know themselves inside-out, so that they can grow up to be self-assured, content and accomplished adults. Thus, most of the anecdotes pertain to children, parenting, and women. They are real-life experiences or snippets from my own counseling sessions and motherhood times.

Secondly, being a good cook; sharing and learning new healthy and quick recipes seemed to be the next spontaneous choice for me.

My husband and I are both travel freaks. With wheels under our feet, as a family, we have traversed the whole length of India (Kashmir to Kerala); the breadth is still pending. Hence a small travelogue narrating my experiences and hoping the reader will visit these off-beat, yet most charming places in my magnificent country.

The above are my secondary pursuits and passions; my primary goal in life is to emulate and become like my spiritual Guru; merge with Him and realize God through him. My life took a U-turn the day I joined meditation with Shri Ram Chandra Mission. I joined the Mission ten years ago, and from that day onwards, I have only changed for the better; a spiritual birth for me.

The first book is dedicated to my Mission; and the path. The second is my journal and learning from the path. The rest will follow in whichever order my whims lead me toward. I hope you like this book and the ones that will follow, and will be able to connect to at least one genre. If any one person is helped through this series I will consider it a humble accomplishment on my part. All the credit goes to my Guru's blessings and the constant strength I receive from my Mission.

Love and joys always,
Sharanya

Foreword:

My heartfelt gratitude to the beloved Master, our guide, for giving me the opportunity to experience the benefits of Sahaj Marg. I take immense pleasure and am filled with joy as I pen the foreword for this very lively book full of experiences which undoubtedly will inspire many seekers to come forward and try this Path, which has transformed us inside out.

Her mention about me saying that I helped her initially, to follow the system rigorously, is not completely true. Instead, seldom do we find such craving in seekers; which makes you want to give all that you have, and if possible, even more. When I did my Masters in Hindi Literature, reading Kabir's literature, I realized that the method of worship I followed as a part of my religious practice, was not real worship, so I started searching for some method that could help me find the goal of life. I practiced Sahaj Marg very rigorously from day one. I found this path after a lot of struggle and many prayers. As a preceptor (trainer) too, whoever came to me to start meditation, I expected the same sort of dedication from them also. Thus, yes, there were times, when I used to force her, when she refused to come forward, like a student of her caliber should have done. I wanted to make her understand and realize the untapped potential she has. My way of delivery is same with all, but not many were able to transform themselves; understand the true goal of life, and be prepared to serve with humility. Gradually, I saw her living life, maturing and inspiring others to do the same. She has become a mentor for some, and tries to help many through her inborn counselling skills.

The Sharanya I saw the first time we met, was a little stiff, firm, introvert, quite rigid and a hard nut to crack. But she was also very simple, keen to learn, a good listener, full of curiosity and eager to know how to lead a purposeful life.

The transformation I could see in her with the practice of Sahaj Marg Meditation; the treasury of jewels which were hidden inside her came to light and started shining; and a new Sharanya, who used to speak only when provoked, is writing this book. The unpolished diamond, today shines through all the cuts. These are not mere words, she has been successful in proving what this path truly is. Sahaj Marg, the path that she is following, and the way she is leading her life; anybody would love to emulate after meeting her.

In her own words, "Today I have better self-awareness, a realistic understanding of who I am and what I want with this life...The drooping face I had when I joined this path has gradually changed into a smiling countenance..... I started this journey in the dark, seeking a silver of light. Today I have the light within me. I am able to setup small light posts and carry this light within me..... This path taught me very gently and peeled the layers revealing a new me to myself. This path is continuously inspiring me to change, know myself better and become extraordinary."

Change as noticed by her husband "When I married her she was Durga astride a lion with a sword in her hand ready to fight at the drop of a hat. Today after joining meditation, she is still Durga, but the sword is gone and her hand now has the "let go" motion; forgiving and moving forward. This is a miracle that has happened right in front of my eyes".

Sahaj Marg is not about getting or gaining something it is about changing and becoming someone.

She has very well proved the efficacy of Sahaj Marg through the transformation she has undergone.

Wishing her success in all her future endeavors.

Affectionately,
Chanderkanta Arora
5th of April 2017.

Contents

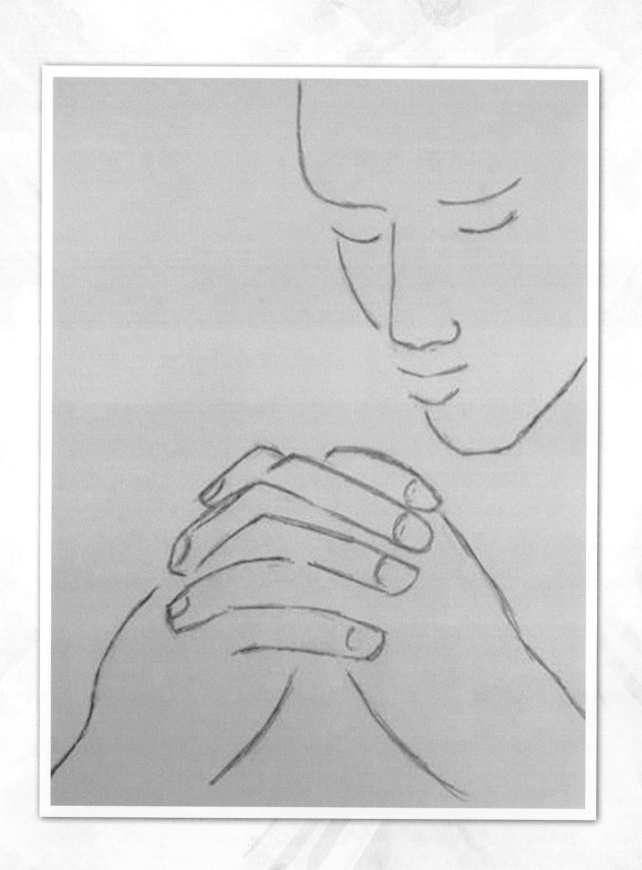

Maxim 1

"Rise before dawn. Offer your prayer and puja (meditation) at a fixed hour preferably before sunrise, sitting in one and the same pose. Have a separate place and seat for worship. Purity of body and mind should be specially adhered to."

I was and still am, a morning person, very used to waking up before dawn. As a teenager, before going to school, my sister and I used to walk to the temple in our vicinity and be the first to offer our prayers. Thus, following this maxim seemed like child's play.

What was a tough nut to crack for many was a piece of cake for me, and thus this was a Maxim which I followed from the day I joined Sahaj Marg.

Like I wrote above, I 'followed' the maxim from the day I joined, and I never faltered or failed in complying with the time table. But much later did I realize the true import of this maxim. The simplicity of this Maxim and this method is what deceived me. Its simplicity is its deception; it all seemed so easy that the profundity escaped me. Out of habit I woke up before dawn, did meditation sitting in the same pose. I always had a Pooja room and a separate place so that also was taken care of. I was doing nothing different and I was very much in my comfort zone.

And, to garnish my spiced ego, most of the abhyasis found this the most challenging maxim. Most of them tried their best, had made multiple attempts, but getting up in the morning was just not their 'cup of tea'. I felt like I had already won half the battle and was ahead of them (Self-improvement was a race for me!). This was the most important maxim, and I was practicing it as recommended, effortlessly. What actual benefit I could have received by following this maxim was lost on me. I compared myself to others and found myself better off. I did not care to dwell on the true purport of this maxim, nor did I introspect to be able to gauge the benefits of practicing this Maxim. Actually, I was defeating the very purpose for which I had joined the Mission, for better self - awareness. I had blissfully covered myself in this best disciple chimerical blanket and continued my abhyaas under this delusion of progress.

In no time though, this getting up in the morning, doing meditation, became ritualistic. It was more out of habit that I was bathing and meditating, rather than out of joy or eager anticipation of what new was awaiting me during my meditation. One morning my husband took a sneak peak and heard me snoring happily in that meditative pose!

He shook me up and said -" instead of getting a cramp or a stiff neck in this pretentious meditation, just sleep, get up fresh and do some constructive meditation. This will do more harm and no good at all."

This was insulting when I first heard it, the comment instantaneously infuriated me and I chastised my well-meaning better half. Upon simmering over that caustic remark for a while, much to my chagrin, I was unable to deny the truth in his observation. I composed my thoughts and with equanimity I weighed over his comment and made 2 changes: I read the book (commentary on 10 Maxims) and tried to understand the maxim, and secondly, I forcibly started to observe myself during meditation, did not give myself a chance to slip, or fall asleep. I used to sit ram - rod straight and be alert; which is what I should have been doing from day one.

My understanding of the Maxim improved after reading the book and I realized I was following everything correctly, but I was merely following some set of instructions. I neither understood the purport nor did I put my heart into it. Probably the answer to why I felt I still had no better self-awareness than when I started this path.

These 10 maxims are very closely connected to one another and set out beautiful guidelines for our daily life, beginning with morning and till the time we retire for the day. So, let me begin with the night prayer, Maxim 10 (this is the maxim which brought the change in me). For my tomorrow to begin on a light and pleasant note, it's imperative that I close my today on a good note.

Maxim 10

"At bedtime, feeling the presence of God, repent for the wrongs committed. Beg forgiveness in a supplicant mood, resolving not to allow repetition of the same."

This is the last Maxim, and we can also say that we are reaching the end of the day. Our 24hours of trying to imbibe His guidelines has come to a close, and our moment of introspection has arrived. This maxim ends our day and seeks His continued guidance for the coming tomorrow.

During the Wednesday satsangh (group meditation), our preceptor (the aspirants appointed by our Guru, who can introduce the new comers to this method) used to ask us "abhyasis" (seekers) to take one maxim at a time for a month and then we abhyasis had to share our understanding about that Maxim. She would ask us to think and introspect as to how much each one of us could imbibe from that Maxim and whether it was easy to follow and practice. She encouraged us to take the Maxim that we thought was the most difficult to follow.

As I mentioned before, the first time I had picked **Maxim 7** : *'Be not revengeful for the wrongs done by others. Take them with gratitude as heavenly gifts.'* I always used to find it very difficult to forgive and forget. If any wrong was done to me all my thoughts and actions were marshaled towards an apt, fitting retaliation which would not just hurt, but kill the adversary. And when two out of ten Maxims (maxim 5 and maxim 7) asked the abhyasis to accept miseries as divine blessings and not to be revengeful of the wrong done by others, I had to do something to bring in that attribute into myself. I had to force myself not to feel vengeful and think negatively about that person who had wronged me. I was unsuccessful till the end of the month because I was continuing to drain my energies thinking bad or ill about the so called 'wrong doers' and had no time to change to become a better person. That one month was probably my longest month because by the end of month I could not honestly tell the preceptor and more importantly, tell myself that I could forgive and forget. I was rather ashamed to say that all my meditation, cleaning, contemplation and repeated affirmations to myself that, 'Yes, I will not be vengeful, I will accept miseries as divine blessings, there is some good hidden for me amongst all the bad that is happening to me...' I was far from feeling less vengeful or vitriolic about people who had wronged me.

This was sometime around the end of December 2008. We were entering into a new year and I was completing a year as an abhyasi. I was yet to perceive a change in myself. Before going to bed that night I fervently prayed to Master (my guru) and was literally crying to help me, help me become a better person, a person with who I could be happy and reconciled. This lack of improvement was persisting, and I wanted to change and maybe for the first time I said my night time prayer exactly the same way we have been asked to do so. I had to feel the presence of God and I did, I put Master right in front of me, sensed His presence and began my prayer.

Tears kept flowing and I said 'sorry' to Him for the last time that night, forgiveness for the wrongs done, knowingly and unknowingly. In a supplicant mood, with absolute humility, on my knees with bent head, really seeking help and promising that I would not repeat my wrongs. I promised myself to change for a better person from that moment and I needed His help, else it was impossible. I was praying for the last 10 months but the essence of the prayer came to me that night. I surrendered and sought His help, 'change me, help me become what You want me to be, I am lost without You.'

Maxim 10 gave me the understanding of the rest of the Maxims. This is the reason my journey of these maxims begins in the reverse order! I started with this Maxim and then was able to begin to live the other 9. Imbibing Maxim 10, practicing it correctly with the exact prescribed attitude helped me follow the rest of the Maxims naturally. Change was a must and change for the better with His help became a step forward. My meditation improved, cleaning was better, my mental state was more composed, and my reactions were proactive, not reactive to the moment or hasty like before. I have travelled a long way now, from that night to today and my bedtime prayer methodology has remained the same, the impact is the same and the result is a very different me.

At times I become lazy or complacent and say my bedtime prayer in a hurry with a 'sorry' to my Master, but I always keep the attitude of humility and think back whether I have yet again done anything that I could have avoided or I may regret tomorrow and the answer is a 'no' so my prayer to Master 'is please help me stay on the right track, give me the discernment to know the right path and thus avoid loopholes and mistakes altogether'.

I could bid adieu to this complacency too the day I heard our new Master's (Kamlesh Patel, fondly referred to as Daaji, is now the president and Heartfulness mediation Master trainer) speech. He said our sadhana involves these 3 steps; *meditation, cleaning and prayer.-*

"*Meditation* is like building our own house; laying a brick one by one every day and you miss any one step there comes a gaping hole, a chasm, in the wall of the house. The number of days you miss the more the number of such schisms. The chances of you creating an unimpaired place for yourself within the spiritual abode.

Cleaning is cleansing your soul. For example, if you place an exposed or uncovered bowl of water for use, by the end of the day the water will become dirty. To avoid this, regular cleaning of the bowl is required so that the water can be used effectively. Likewise, throughout the day, we are exposed to all good and bad experiences. Whatever negative thoughts or actions that you did in a day, think of those, realize them, accept your mistakes while cleaning. Through regular cleaning your soul would be purified and be rid of "samskara" (impressions) and bad habits like ego, fear, superstition, anger, and many others in the same genre.

Prayer is an absolute surrender to the Master. The morning prayer before we begin our day (as an invitation to receive the grace), and the same prayer (with a totally different attitude) at bedtime, before we retire for the day".

This wonderful Mission opens its arms wide and accepts one and all, the place we abhyasis choose to reside in is left to us. My understanding of the three M's- the Master, Mission and Method helped me begin this awesome journey fruitfully. It has taught and changed me for better.

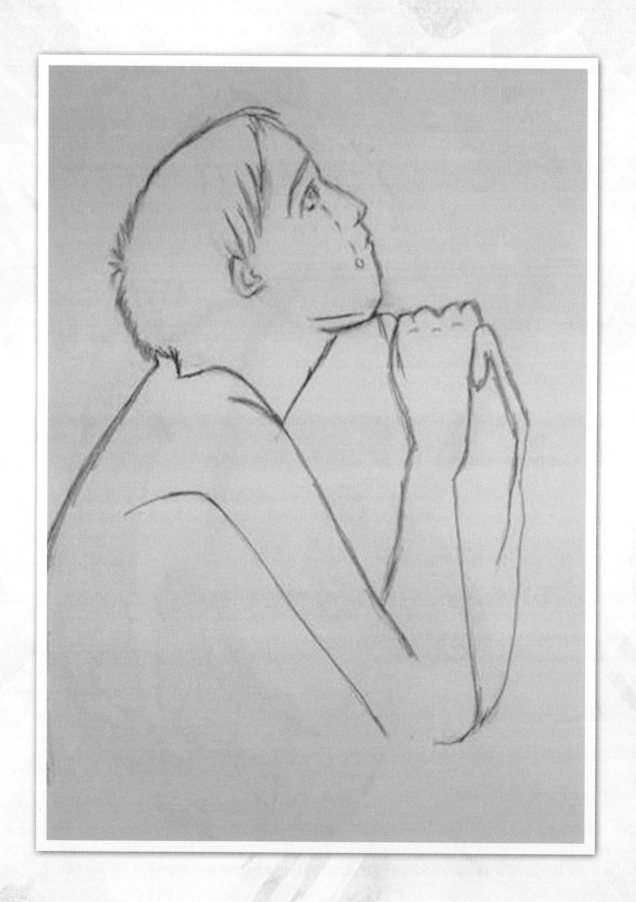

Maxim 1; again

... for my tomorrow to begin on a light and pleasant note, it's imperative that I close my today on a good note.

Our night prayer should be with an attitude of surrender, trying to talk to our God within, and seeking forgiveness for day's mistakes; and His help in making our tomorrows better. Thus, at night, we pray to Him, seeking His help and stay connected to Him.

He helps us in our sleep, in our semi-conscious state and we wake up before dawn (our first Maxim) finish our morning ablutions and make an attempt to reconnect to Him. We re - convene where we left off the previous night and continue our conversation with our God within. That one hour of meditation is again our time with Him, where we plan to stay connected to Him through the day.

Why before dawn? Dawn is the time when the night meets the day, and the nature is at its best 'giving' mood. Grace flows in abundance and meditating is beneficial and progressive. It is also the ideal time when there are no external disturbances. Our mind and body are fresh, in sync and in complete harmony with the environment around. There is also a feeling of peace and tranquility around us. Also, it is the most auspicious hour of the day.

Beginning my day with meditation keeps me charged, energetic and fresh through the entire day. That one hour of meditation is like my battery recharging hour or my intake of positive energy pills that pull me through the day's challenges. If by chance I skipped my morning meditation, my day always seemed to drag, and I lacked the zest and ardor. My mood would be mercurial, and my outbursts would be more.

My other personal experience was; postponing this morning time to some other time during the day did not sit well with me. This was my time, my one hour of introspective, ruminative time. If I sacrificed this, the rest of the day also became unfruitful. At times, due to some pressing reasons, I tried sitting for meditation at a later time, but my mind was cluttered and totally absorbed with thoughts of myself and the errands I had to run. The peaceful self which was in tune with my mind and body during the wee hours of the morning was missing in the later part of the day. And as the day progressed many mundane works and thoughts like an absent domestic help, what to cook for a meal, any irrelevant disagreement would hamper my meditation. Hence, an entire hour passed by with no 'my time' at all. With so much already occupying my mind I do not enjoy meditating during the day. Thus, the dawn remained my ideal time, where I am at peace and totally with my Self.

Thus, everything fell in place and change did happen once I followed the Maxim with the right attitude, absolute understanding and with an ardent desire for self-improvement. I begin my day with meditation, and at the right time and in the same place too, as advised. We humans are creatures of habit. And in asking us to meditate in the same place, Master was trying to form a good habit for us. Sitting in the same place, same time helped me block, shoo away the irrelevant distractions very easily. The minute I enter my meditation room my body and mind both seem to acknowledge the fact that the coming 90 minutes are 'my time'. Very soon I was able to meditate and enjoy meditation, observe myself, write my diary and compare my notes. This takes me to the next Maxim now... I begin my meditation with prayer...

Maxim 2

"Begin your pooja (meditation) with a prayer for spiritual elevation with a heart full of love and devotion."

For me, this Maxim was always a continuation of Maxim 1. The way getting up early was a part of my habit, reciting Gayatri Mantra was also a habit I practiced very diligently. In retrospect, I realize that I never really gave much thought to any Maxim. Upon a cursory reading I found almost all of them very easy. So, the perusal never happened. I felt I was already following all of them and I did not have to put in any extra effort to imbibe them, or allow them to become integral to me, not as a part of my daily regimen, but as my second nature. Apart for the 7ᵗʰ Maxim; that instantaneously scared me, the rest were not very different from how I was presently leading my life.

My over confidence got the better of me. Sadly, it took me years to understand, imbibe and start to live by them.

Our Prayer is a simple four lines. Parroting these four lines absent-mindedly, takes barely half a second. My morning meditation always began with prayer, an absent minded, half a second utterance, ensued by meditation. The day I started to understand and pay closer attention to Maxim 1, I began to introspect and search the true meaning in the rest of the Maxims too. Maxim 1 had eluded me for two years and I was now more prudent. These purportedly simple maxims were not so simple after all. So, what was the second Maxim telling me and was I really following it the way it was intended?

"Begin your pooja (meditation) with a prayer for spiritual elevation... I was reciting the prayer but not for Spiritual elevation. I was yet to know my spiritual goal, so elevating in that goal would have to wait. So, I gently came to the second part of this one liner Maxim, *with a heart full of love and devotion."* Could that hasty half a second, perfunctory murmuring of four lines equate to 'reciting *with a heart full of love and devotion'*? Neither was my heart there nor was any devotion involved. I was clueless about my Spiritual Goal, so elevation of that elusive Goal was also equally far-fetched.

Our prayer is to be said with the intent of establishing a relationship or connection with the Divine within. When I started Sahaj Marg I was not in a state where I could really identify and say, 'yes! This is what I want'! Or 'This is exactly what I seek, this is my goal'. My entry was a desperate attempt to salvage my sinking self. I wanted to know myself and where I was headed. My first year on this path, I spent trying to figure out myself and where I stood in the whole scheme of things.

The prayer begins thus,

"O Master!

Thou art the Real Goal of human Life...

This "O Master!" and the attitude of calling out to Him, the Divine within, should be such that I 'connect' to the Divine. The night prayer was seeking His help in a supplicant mode. The same prayer had a different attitude and feel to it in the morning. I call out once and stay connected. So, the call had to have the depth, sincerity and longing in it! One knock, one ring and He is forced to listen, and open the doors of my heart, and be seated! Be with me for that one hour of meditation and continue to be by my side through the day. My present goal was to stay connected, spiritual elevation was to follow later, after I had perfected this connection part.

I was slowly trying to become Like Him, and then become Him. I had started this journey as three different entities; one was me, the seeker or beggar. Second was God, the creator, who I was appealing to, seeking help from to make me self-aware; and finally, the third was My Guru, I was following the path, method given by him and thus He was my teacher, hand holding me and leading me towards the Creator. Through Meditation the difference between God and guru disappeared and a day came when I uttered "O'Master!" and I was verily calling out to my guru, welcoming Him into my heart so that we could have our tete-a-tete before I began my day. Over the years, I have now come to discern the goal of this remaining life, the remaining two entities had to become one. God-Guru and I had to merge, that was the "Real Goal"

Thus, I began the day with Meditation, which began with a prayer to My Master, for spiritual elevation. And I had to pray just once, not parrot it mindlessly, but whole heartedly and brimming with love and devotion, so that He is forced to come, and I stay connected to him through the day.

Incidentally, in my morning prayer I could focus on the first two lines of the prayer,

"O Master!

Thou art the Real Goal of human Life.

And, when it was time for my bedtime prayer-meditation my focus somehow shifted to the last two lines; when I invariably recollected my day's events and checked where I had faltered, again. So, I kept seeking His help in making amends, help in changing myself for the better, help to work on me through the night so that I become who He wants me to become.

"We are yet but slaves of wishes, putting bar to our advancement.

Thou art the only God and power to bring us up to that stage."   Now, before beginning my morning meditation, I close my eyes and pray, just once, with a heart full of love and devotion. I earnestly seek His presence by my side, wait for him to hold my hand and ensure that I step out of the meditation room along with Him. I spend the hour with Him, in my meditation room, sometimes at peace, soaking it all up, at times busy exchanging some notes, asking some doubts and on some days, I have a long list of complaints. My eagerness to be with Him increases every day and if due to some unforeseen reason, I miss my morning meditation the whole day slips by in a state of restlessness and irritation. Finally, I was hopeful that I understood this Maxim and was trying to practice it in its true essence.

I was ready to learn about Maxim 3 now...

Maxim 3

"Fix your Goal which should be complete oneness with God. Rest not till the ideal is achieved."

As I started to understand the other Maxims, I became aware of how superficial my understanding really was. A*bhyaas* lifted my veil of ignorance and my attempts to fathom the true import of these Maxims became earnest. I now know that to follow them, I have to live them, make them a part of my life. Since then, every day my learning has improved, and a new facet of the same Maxim revealed itself to me. The best part of these Maxims is that all of them are worded positively. They are simple suggestions of how we can conduct our daily life. They could be compared to small guiding lights on this spiritual journey, throwing light on the road ahead and removing a few road blocks if the aspirant succeeds in following them willingly. As my awareness grew, the spirit of enquiry also bloomed, and I felt encouraged to discover more and hasten this journey of discovering the true meaning of these Maxims.

This journey was purely tailor made for me, (for every seeker). There is no one to compete with, but myself, no one to be better than, but myself. I am allowed to move at my pace, with my willingness and my efforts. Thus, this Maxim took me through many turns; many small milestones which egged me on my onward journey towards achieving the real or "The Ultimate Goal". I learnt the subtle difference between ambition and aspiration. My ambitious goals gradually altered and became my aspirations on this spiritual adventure. He kept showing me the Ultimate Goal, His goal for all of us. On this self- discovering spiritual journey, I tried to set up my milestones, always keeping in focus my Ultimate Goal.

Today, I have better self-awareness, a realistic understanding of who I am, and what I want with my life. My biggest grouse of being educated unemployed is gone. I am still unemployed, but the unemployed status is by choice and I am happy with it. I still get this creepy feeling of stepping out and doing some work, but not with the intent of being employed and working to earn, but with the intent of being constructively useful to someone. I feel it is my responsibility to serve or give back to the society in whatever little capacity I can. Moreover, I aspire to put my learning to use. Pass my learnings to someone and learn more through teaching. This is the inclination with which I continue to search for venues to serve or work. Being educated did not necessarily mean I had to be employed. This change in my thinking brought many positive changes.

I could feel the transformation, a metamorphosis occurring within me. My expectations from others disappeared. A relationship suffers the most because of unmet expectations. Thus, with this simple change of having no expectations, I have been able to build better relationships. My grudges and resentments are on their exit journey. My ability to express or articulate myself honestly has improved. I am a much braver person today. As a house wife, I never had the confidence or the self-reliance that I could accomplish anything on my own. I always looked at others for support or help. Today, I am content and have the self-assurance that I can accomplish anything I set my mind to. I am self–reliant and confident in my own place. My comparison with other achievers and go -getters has ceased. I can now figure out when and what will make me angry and I am able to combat my anger before it causes any harm and in the interim, I have learnt to fight my battles alone. Reaching these small milestones has made me emotionally free. The boost to my confidence has egged me on to seek ventures where I can help others. The drooping sad face I had when I joined this Path has gradually evolved into a smiling countenance. The feeling that the whole world was against me and conspiring to trap me, has now changed. Today, the world is with me and is goading me to accomplish my goals and help me realize my own true worth! I started this journey in the dark, seeking a sliver of light. Today, I have the light within me. I am able to set up small light posts and carry this light within me. I have to become the ball of light that attracts others towards this light. This small flickering flame has the strength of a candle light, lighting other candles as it burns itself. Soon enough, these small candle lights will merge together and become a flaming torch.

My Master ended one of His talks with just two words, *'Be contagious'*. These words keep echoing and I long to put my best foot forward, give this Mission all I have, and 'become contagious'!

Maxim 4

"Be plain and simple to be identical with Nature"

From this Maxim onwards, we move from our individual *sadhana (daily practice)* to things outside of our individual self. The first 3 maxims focus on the aspirant and help the aspirant to introspect. Our individual *sadhana* is meant for us to become more self-aware, contemplative, discerning and enable us to connect to the Divine within.

The next four Maxims (4, 5, 6, and 7) are on our interaction with the world outside; beginning with the Nature. At the risk of sounding repetitive and boring I am forced to say that the simplicity of these Maxims fooled me yet again. Apart for Maxim 7, I never did pay much attention to any other Maxim. I was arrogant or rather more ignorant about myself and studied the Maxims with a casual perspective, patting my back and thinking that I already had these attributes in me and I was thus practicing and naturally living all the other Maxims! What was there to imbibe or learn beyond this was my thinking. Fortunately for me, my failure to imbibe Maxim 7 forced me to take a closer look at the other Maxims. I started to revisit every Maxim with greater care and pondered deep. These maxims which are merely one line in length and in a seemingly simple language, had great profundity and were taking me months to really fathom and years to put them into practice. Furthermore, when I finally did muster the courage and confidence to think that I could tick off a maxim and would give it a final confirmatory perusal, some new meaning would reveal itself and I would be busy trying to understand the Maxim again, afresh!

I thought myself as a 'simple' person but to be 'simple and identical with Nature' did not cross my mind. When I read this Maxim the only quality which I attributed to Nature was self-less giving. For me being akin to nature meant to give, give without expectation. Nature never seeks a thank you, or a favor in return for all that She gives us. We relentlessly abuse it and yet she ceaselessly gives.

Till I did not read about Bade Ghulam Ali Khan, I used to think of myself as a giving, generous person. My bloated self-image got punctured considerably after reading this:

Bade *Ghulam Ali Khan, the famous ghazal singer, was known to give, give and give. He returned home to Pakistan, preferring to spend the last days of his life in his homeland. But his Indian Bhajans and songs in praise of Indian Gods was met with opposition; forcing him to return to Bombay, India. He came back a penniless man with no income or wealth. So, his aficionados, the lovers of his music, collected Rs. 20000/- (In those days it was decent amount) and gifted the sum to the virtuoso.*

That very evening, after the concert; somebody came up to Ghulam Ali Saab and started weeping, saying he had no money, not even for food. This great human being pulled out the entire sum of Rs. 20000/- from his pockets and simply gave it all to the weeping person! He retained not a single coin even.

Here I was, thinking of myself as a giving person. Yet, if I had to put some money into the donation box, I used to search for hours and dig out the lowest denomination possible. Not a coin; (that would be below my dignity) but a note, decent enough to make me look dignified in front of others, and low enough not to pinch my pocket too much! Hypocrisy at its shrouded best is how I would succinctly put it. This anecdote inspired me to try and consciously cultivate this attribute in myself; to give always, give without expectation and be able to give without a loss to self also.

This path helped me see so many flaws in myself. The way the mind works and deceives if it is left to its own resources, continuously came to light. Why the seers of the old implored us to 'listen to the heart'. Why every Sage finally ended up on the doorstep of 'meditation' was becoming clear to me.

Nature was more than merely giving though. The explanation of this Maxim begins with; *"Simplicity is the very essence of Nature. It can aptly be described as the quintessence of the ultimate.......* ends with these lines; *Try to re-own the latent power which is the very quintessence of Nature of breaking up the network interwoven by yourself."*

These lines gave the Maxim many meanings. Giving was a natural thing for Nature, it knew nothing else. To be like Nature meant much more than giving. Nature is the same inside out. To become a reflection of Nature, akin to Nature I had to become pure, not just giving. Nature is God because of its purity, God is pure. Nature has borne and withstood the ravages of time. We have defaced it and abused it beyond recognition and yet it remains as it is, plain and simple.

Simplicity teaches us surrender, acceptance, patience, love without expectation, duty, giving; oneness or becoming one. Amidst diversity, colour and differences Nature admirably translates this unique attribute of Oneness, of progress and growth together.

Nature grows on its own, with the help of rain and sunshine. But it blossoms and bears fruit only if it is nurtured and tended to with love and in the right environment. Nature needs no help to grow, a seed becomes a tree and fulfils its duty of giving shade to travellers, wood for homes, food to animals and fruit for us. We need to do nothing, nor does it seek any help. But if we want the best from Nature, a conscious effort is imperative. Similarly, I could become a better person walking on this path and making a short de-tour on and off and coming back to track again. This continued wandering and being pulled back in the right direction did help me, but to be in 'tune with Nature' I had to learn caution.

To help us, Nature annihilates and causes destruction, gets rid of the excesses and brings normalcy or balance. It is not always giving, accepting or surrendering. Nature shows anger and rebellion too! It cannot sustain adulteration nor bear the burden of impurities for long. It becomes destructive and goes on a rampage to salvage its own purity and then return to its original state. This was a new learning for me.

Nature was both, creative and destructive but with always One goal, retaining its Purity. This purity weaved its destiny. Consistent awareness and conscious efforts to retain the good, get rid of the bad, stay balanced, become pure and be able to project one singular persona, as within so outside; this was an uphill task.

I am on the road to becoming 'simple and in tune with Nature'; when I confidently feel, I have become so, then I will rewrite this Maxim. Till then suffice to say I have tried to understand it, thanks to my Guru. I am on my journey to becoming one with it too...

Moving on to the next Maxim now,

Maxim 5

"Be truthful. Take miseries as Divine Blessings for your own good and be thankful."

The second part of this Maxim I will not (I cannot) elucidate here. I did not read the second part of this Maxim with the first part. The second section's learning came to me with my most oft repeated maxim, Maxim 7! In this Maxim I was always reading just the first two words, *'Be Truthful'* and what a roller coaster ride these two words took me on is what I can truthfully narrate here. I could never get around to understanding the rest of the Maxim.

This experience with my daughter probably explains these two words ideally:

My daughter (then 9 years old) sees only 'black and white' in everything. She has no shades of grey in her thought process nor in her actions. Everything is either true or false, it cannot be half-true or 'simply said so' 'did not mean it to be a lie' none of this worked with her. Her innocence, incessant cross questioning and maddeningly hair-splitting scrutiny of every word I utter has forced me to be vigilant and weigh my words with utmost care and caution. Resultantly, loose talk is completely out of bounds in my house!

There are innumerable incidents in my daily life and every anecdote has some learning for me and I realize that I may have imparted very little of me to the kids whereas my learning from them has been unimaginable!

We learn music together; my daughter and I. she is an amazing singer, more like a child prodigy and I am just the opposite. To be brutally honest, I really don't know why I am still in the class, because my vocal chords seem to be the same and my voice worse than ever. For some strange reason I continued to go and never thought of quitting. It is such a contrasting scene in the class; ma'am asked both of us to sing a particular Raga and my daughter received this compliment, "It is the teacher's good fortune and good karma that they get a chance to teach such and gifted, natural and exemplary student." I was all smiles and feeling very proud when she smilingly added, "Sharanya, you don't feel bad, whatever you lack and can never achieve; God has bestowed on your daughter in a double doze!!"I said nothing; simply smiled.

Recently, because of unprecedented spate of visitors I was too over worked and decided to skip a few classes. The first 2 classes the teacher did not ask about my whereabouts and my daughter also never bothered to find out why I was not accompanying her. Third class, the teacher asked her, and she very innocently replied, "She just dropped me off and returned home ma'am, don't know why!!"

When she told me, I didn't know what to say!! What would the teacher think? I was returning from her door step the last 3 classes!! God!! This silly girl, she could have lied or made some excuses on my behalf!!

And as fate would have it I could not go for the next class either. But I carefully coached my girl and told her to tell ma'am, in case she asked, that I was unwell. That is why I am not attending the class.

I eagerly waited for her return that day, totally restless and praying that she would not mess up. The minute she returned I asked her if ma'am had enquired. She was very upset and took off like a rocket saying, "Please give me a complete reason next time!! What exactly has happened to you? I don't know!"

I was a bit taken aback at her angry outburst and asked, "What exactly occurred, baby? What did ma'am ask?"

Daughter, "She asked me why you did not come and like you said I told her that you were unwell!"

Me "Then?"

Daughter "Then what! She asked what exactly happened to you! And I don't know what is wrong with you, so what could I say?"

"Then, what did you say?"

"All I could say was, I don't know what is wrong with her, but I heard her taking an appointment with the doctor now and I know that she is going to a doctor in a while", and she continued very sweetly, " Please give full details next time !! I hate lying"

I felt very bad for her and totally ashamed that I was not only forcing her to lie, but encouraging it as well. What was a casual habit for me, making excuses, became a grave lie for her and she could not cope with that burden. I apologized to her and promised myself that I would never repeat anything like this again.

That incident was the catalyst, I am a changed person today. I am regular for class, no excuses. Not only did I stop lying I went a step further and questioned the veracity of my reason or excuse too.

I am more of an introvert and hate to step out of the comfort zone. Any invitation to attend a party or a get together sent my head spinning in search of plausible excuses. I could never boldly say 'no' for the fear of hurting that person or for the fear of never being invited in the future (Then I would be very lonely, which was not what I wanted!). I needed a viable 'reason' for my absence which kept my social image untarnished. Thus, till the last minute I used to commit to the engagement and at the eleventh hour drop off by putting the blame on my poor unaware husband or making an excuse about some non - existent last minute unavoidable engagement. However, the guilt became too heavy and I could not carry this weight any longer. Finally, I mustered the courage to tell them that I wanted to be invited, but I may not attend any of these functions. I reassured them that it was not any fault of theirs, but my inherent nature was thus. Being an understanding group of friends they understood me completely. I still get invited and if I don't choose to go, I say so. I have no reason to lie. I go if I am comfortable else I say I won't be coming. This small change has made me feel so free, unburdened and light.

Even in my daily interactions with my husband the application of these two words brought a sea of change. I usually avoid confrontations or arguments. Peace has to be maintained at all costs was and is still my motto in life. However in the past, maintaining this 'pseudo peace' made me avoid many altercations and hide many facts from my husband. Whatever I assumed he may disagree with or would not like, I never brought it to his notice. If he inquired about some incidents, I kept silent or looked side-ways. There came a time when I was trying to keep track of what I had told him and what excuses I made and which excuse had I given for what. Finally, I hung my boots here too! Honesty seemed the simplest route to take. I tell him as it is and much to my surprise he never says anything! It was all in my head and I was unnecessarily imagining things . He comments wherever he thinks necessary and I honestly do a cross check and make the changes. This was so simple! I am truthfully at peace now, and the peace at home is also for real.

Such small things really, and I was uselessly complicating my life and overworking my brain thinking of excuses and lies, where none were necessary. These little incidents have changed my approach towards my life, and the learning I received is very humbling. Being truthful has simplified my life, earned me more respect in my own eyes and I have earned the implicit faith and trust of one and all. Letting go of one quality has earned me many new attributes.

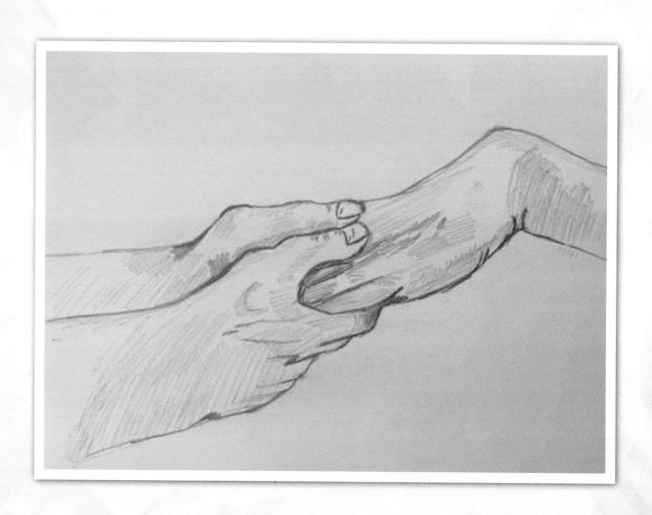

Maxim 6

"Know all people as thy brethren and treat them as such"

My journey with this maxim began with no goal in mind. It was a mindless search which gradually progressed into having a goal....an individual goal of self- betterment.

I think the best way to trace my journey to the present understanding of this Maxim can be described through my state of mind with which I attended our Annual Congregations. Since I have traversed this journey over a period of 5 years I will briefly describe my state of mind during these gatherings and how I finally have a semblance of an understanding of this maxim. I joined this Path in 2008 and participated in my first Annual Congregation (I will call it *'Bhandara'* because that is how we refer to our spiritual gatherings.)

The celebration of our spiritual Master's birthday is called *'Bhandara'*. Celebrating our Master's Birthday is a way of coming together under one roof, rejoicing and partaking of the Divine grace, which is present during such auspicious occasions and one gains immense spiritual benefit . When I joined, we used to have 3 such celebrations. One was in February, Basant Panchmi Day, our Adi Guru's birthday. The second came in April end which was our second Guru, Babuji Maharaj's birthday and the third one followed in July, our then /living Master, Rajgopalachari Parthsarthi's birthday. Since, 2015 we have the joy of being able to meet four times, the fourth one being our Fourth and present guru's Kamlesh Patel's Birthday in September. The gathering is very huge with almost 40000 and more abhyasis attending from all over the world.

Initially, I could attend only one *Bhandara* per annum because of my family commitments. I would eagerly wait for this chance and make the most out of it. These *Bhandaras* would be my revitalising pills for the whole year and I would be gluttonous for whatever I could grab at; my soul arsenal to last me for a year.

My first *Bhandara* was a teaser and left me hungry for more. It was not what I had expected or imagined, but I longed to be a part of every Bhandara henceforth. First I had to live up to the mission statement of this path "Meditation for Self- Realization", which I continue to do with utmost sincerity. The journey of self- realization unravelled itself ever so gently from my next *Bhandara*.

July 2010- I was ecstatic about this trip. It had come after a long wait. Finally, I was attending a *Bhandara.* My sole focus was the Mission statement "Meditation for Self- Realization", and that was my plan. My intentions were very self-centred and selfish, I was going there for me and me alone! I attended every single *satsangh*. We had 3 *satsangh* everyday; 6:30 AM was the first, then 11:00 AM and then in the evening the last one was at 5:00 PM.

I woke up at 3:00 AM, in an attempt to escape the morning rush near the wash area. By 3:45 AM I finished my morning ablutions and reached my tent. Then I did my morning meditation, for about 50 minutes to an hour, in a state of absolute peace with myself. I finished writing my diary and headed towards the canteen for a fresh cup of coffee. By 5:15 AM, I walked towards the meditation hall soaking in the fresh air and the morning hustle bustle around me. Just before entering the meditation hall I called my family back home. Once inside the meditation hall, I happily settled in a corner with a good view of my beloved Master. I chose an ideal spot which was in the front row, from where I could see my Master walk on to the stage. From 5:15 to 6:30 in the morning, it was waiting time.

I did not have the heart to do much after the first *satsangh*. So, at leisure, I wrote my diary, collected my thoughts, stretched my feet, got rid of my cramps and strolled towards the canteen. I had breakfast in solitude and enjoyed watching the crowd. By 9:30 a.m. I sat down for the second *Satsangh*. Each day after the second *satsangh*, I would explore the entire premises.

The *Bhandara* premises is spread over acres and is a good 10-minute walk from the comfortable dormitory to the meditation hall. They have a photograph gallery, with photos on display, and for sale. The displayed photos showcase the entire journey of Sahaj Marg right from its inception to the Global presence it enjoys today. Babuji handed over the baton to my Master in 1983, and over the last 40 years Master has breathed life into it. All this is portrayed aesthetically in the Gallery section.

The second day I wandered around in the book stall. All the old publications and the new releases of this year were on display and for sale. All the speeches that Master has given over the years are compiled into books for the benefit of the abhyasis.

The last day we had one *Satsangh* in the morning and the closing event of the *Bhandara* was a heart warming speech by the Master. I returned home satiated yet craving for more, smiling because I had finally attended a *Bhandara* and got teary eyed as I had to go back home. This place felt like home. Those 3 days were my happiest days and I wanted them to go on. Apart for the perfunctory duty call in the morning, the thought of home, children, and domestic routines never came to my mind. Thus, in 2010 July *Bhandara*, I was seriously working on myself, for myself.... purely a selfish person who is voracious for more self-awareness.

My next Bhandara came in July 2011. This *Bhandara* was different in many ways. I attended with the whole family. Since, my husband had recently started practice, and I was eager for him to derive utmost benefit. I wanted him to experience what I had experienced last year.

Unfortunately, it did not go as I had imagined. The weather that year was suffocating and hot. Moreover, heavy downpour increased the humidity unbearably. The crowd was way beyond the expected number and the whole place was chaotic. All my hopes and expectations came crashing down, the children kept complaining about the heat. My husband and children wanted to shift to a hotel. He was amazed that how could anyone meditate in such heat and suffocation. He decided to sit in the air-conditioned comfort of his car and meditate which was blasphemous for me, but I was helpless!

Thus, this *Bhandara* gave me a very different experience. I was eager to return home. The family was not having a good time and their discomfort was making me unhappy and miserable. I was caught between attending to my daughter in the hotel and running back to attend my satsangh. I was more than happy to head home after the last *satsangh*. Despite everything happening against my wishes I was able to maintain my calm and equanimity. There was a change in my approach and thinking, I graciously accepted or accommodated my interests despite everything going against my will and wish. My wait for the next *Bhandara* began even before I properly bid adieu to this one.

July 2012 *Bhandara,* I went alone. My husband opted to stay at home and look after the children. This year my mind set was different. I realized that I did not come for the ambrosial shower. I noticed that this year I wanted to be a deserving disciple, worthy of His grace. All these years I had done nothing for the Mission. This time I wanted to serve, I wanted to reach out and embrace every other abhyasi and do some work and be constructively useful to the organization. I felt guilty attending *satsangh*, eating, loitering and again attending *satsangh* without contributing in anything. This was definitely not what Master would have wanted from an old abhyasi. This was the year that I noticed all the banners and hoardings in the *Bhandara*; they all read "Meditation for Human Integration", and it was time I also participated in the larger goal.

I still have a long way to go before I can confidently say that I consider everyone as my brethren. However, I have graduated ever so subtly from groping in the dark to better self –awareness, to wanting to play a role in human integration. Today, I know that every single person who crosses my path has a reason, and the reason is for my good. I had to be patient, accept and learn. This change happened inside me, without my conscious awareness and without any effort on my part. I have definitely become daring enough to challenge my own limitations and correct myself. Today I am bold enough to look at the mirror and strive for perfection. I am willingly participating and surrendering to whatever comes my way. My Master says, *"When we are marching on this path of God, even loss turns out to be profit."—Pearls of Wisdom by Ramchandra ji of Shahjahanpur*

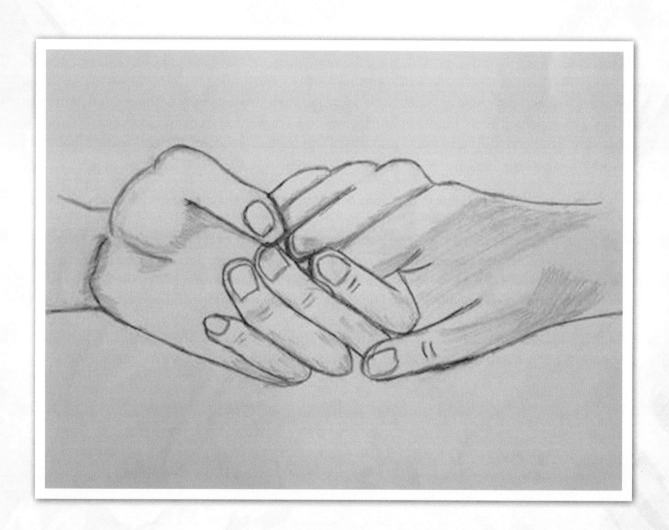

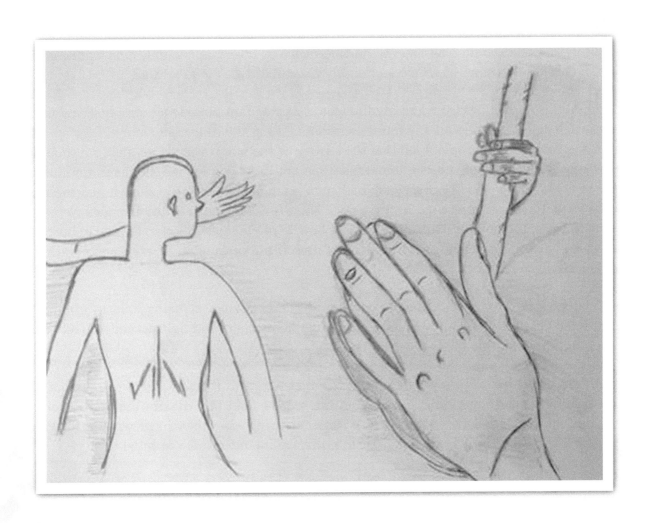

Maxim 7

"Be not revengeful for wrongs done by others. Take them with gratitude as heavenly gifts."

This is still my toughest Maxim. Even a cursory reading of this Maxim raised my hackles and I found it very incredulous. It was impossible for me to comprehend the second part of the Maxim. Even if I did consider for a minute, imbibing and succeeding in putting the first part to practice, *"Be not revengeful for wrongs done by others."* the second part was an absolute bouncer! The expectation that one should *"consider these wrongs done by others as heavenly gifts and be grateful for them."* This was extremely bizarre and highly unrealistic for me to fathom.

I had joined this Path at a stage when my life was at its stagnant best. I was simply living my life allowing each day to slip through my fingers without making any impact or change. I had so many grudges against so many people. I felt that the burden of the world was on my delicate shoulders, I was wronged by everyone, no one understood me and stood up for me, not even my husband nor my very own kith and kin. Everyone had some agenda against me and each had their own personal vendetta dossier prepared in my name! Thus, most of my time and energies were spent in trying to figure out how to get back at them or how to prove myself better, or how to beat them at their own game. Needless to say, I was giving myself importance in a very undermining and self-deprecative way.

Thus, reading this Maxim and accepting my prefect's challenge of being able to imbibe this Maxim in the coming one month was like climbing the Everest. I did not succeed, in fact I failed miserably in imbibing this Maxim.

I actually put this Maxim in my Pandora's box for 2 years and focused on other maxims. This maxim simply seemed impossible to me. And the more I read this maxim the more I felt that Master definitely would have intended to write something else, may have wanted to word it differently. This was definitely not what He would have intended us to imbibe!

Two years later when I finally mustered the courage to read this Maxim again; the explanation to this Maxim starts off thus: *"Almost all religions unanimously agree that whatever happens is a result of our actions. Nobody ever suffers in contravention of this principle. ....Truly speaking, we ourselves are the makers of our fate."*

These lines kept reiterating the fact that what was happening to me was somewhere connected to me and me alone. Consciously or sub-consciously I had done something to trigger the spate of events and I was justifiably reaping the fruit of what I had sown. Now, what had I sown, and when? I was unaware of it. And the fact that these wrongs that were happening to me were in verity my own doing was a very irritating truth, a bitter pill to swallow. It took me two years to re-open this Maxim, and I was just finding my bearings now.

This is what follows next, *"As a rule, Nature wants to keep everything crystal and pure just as it had originally come down in the beginning. Even the slightest coating veils its lustre."*

These lines gave me a better insight. I did join meditation because I wanted to change and know myself better. Meditation was also repeatedly telling me that until I did not learn to look at the mirror and really 'see' myself, things and events would continue to repeat themselves. This adulterated me was never going to go anywhere, in this impure state. So, the purification had to happen. I had to pay up for what I had done. In other words, I had to clean the slate, otherwise even the smallest speck of dust and dirt would veil the lustre and my journey towards my goal would be futile.

I had cemented the goal within myself (Maxim 3); I was aspiring for a merger, nothing less. How can anything impure merge with the pure? I had to pay off these debts and the sooner the better. They were anyway my doings and deeds of the past whether from this birth or previous births I had no idea. So, it would be in my best interest if I tried not to be revengeful of the wrongs done by others! They were in fact helping me repay my debts and clearing my slate. A little calm introspection revealed that they were hastening me forward on my spiritual journey and towards my ultimate goal. I had to be thankful to them! They were indeed heavenly gifts and blessings in disguise.

Our tendencies or inner characteristics are our inherent nature and extremely strong and deep rooted. Any unpleasant incident or even a small provocation, our tendencies raise their ugly head. Tendencies are like a riverbed, always wet and soaking. As the level of water increases, the river bed gets muddier, thicker and more slippery. I am consciously trying to dry up the riverbed by trying to get rid of some of these tendencies. Freeing myself of tendencies is like having a spell of rain in the river bed and not expecting it to turn muddy. It is said that these tendencies repeat themselves over and over again, like the devil showing its temptations and the poor angel trying hard to resist all the time! My efforts were of the poor angel here, successfully resisting 10 times and the 11th time I succumb, and the river is in floods again and alas, I am back to square one!

I am unable to conquer this Maxim even with better insight and understanding. Many nuances still elude me, and I keep slipping and getting up all the time. This maxim has become like that game of snakes and ladders for me. I put in all my will power and climb up to the 98th house and the huge snake bites me and I seem to slip into the 3rd house again. It is a fresh start all over and this continues still.

Thankfully, my meditation has helped me understand the meaning and relevance of this Maxim. Master has worded it exactly the way it should have been worded. I am trying not to be revengeful of wrongs done by others. And, I do acknowledge that they are heavenly gifts, and I accept them with utmost humility and gratitude.

Maybe I can understand the next maxim too, whilst I continue to work on this one. This one may be work-in-progress for a while.

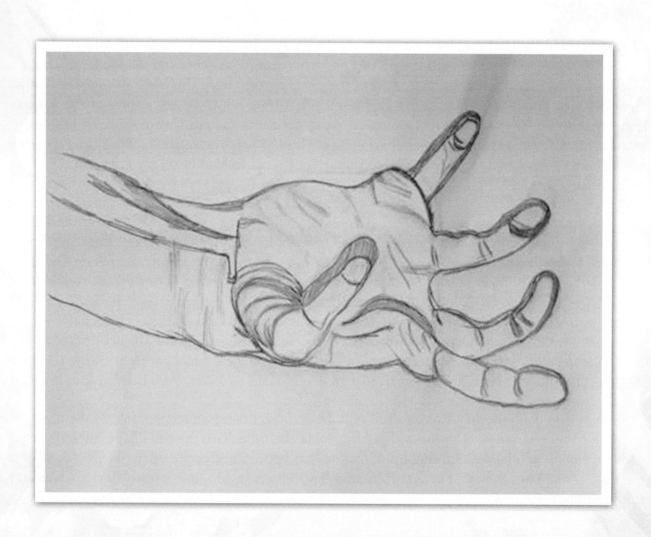

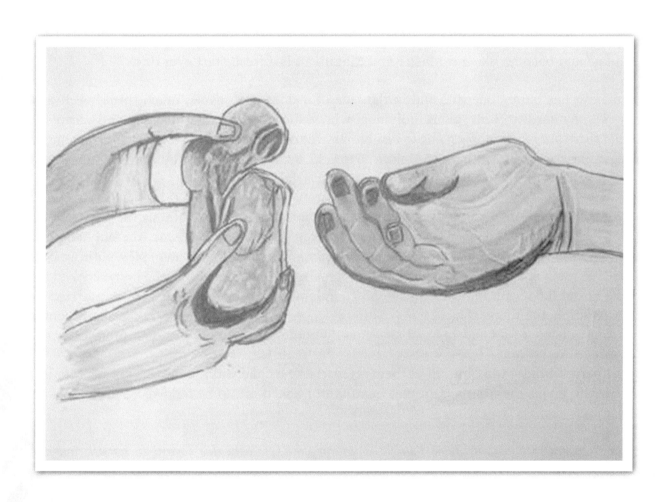

MAXIM 8

*"Be happy to eat in constant divine thought whatever you get,
with due regard to honest and pious earnings"*

Of the 10 maxims, this is the only Maxim on food. The first 3 are on our individual sadhana; the next four (Maxim-4-5-6-7) are based on our interaction with nature, family and society. Maxim 8 is on the food we eat, and the affect it has on us. Why a particular kind of food is advised and why we should preferably stay away from some kinds of food. Maxim 9 is our end goal, trying to emulate and become like our Master and Maxim 10 is a fresh start ever day.

This maxim has barely one line and in the face of it does not invoke much thinking. It looks simple for any hard working, pious individual who values food and feels blessed and accepts the fact that there are more people going to bed hungry than with people who are fortunate enough to partake a hearty meal. All that the Maxim says is to eat what is offered by thanking the creator for enabling us with the good fortune to be able to partake the food.

As a student, hostel life had totally frozen my taste buds and I was one among the very few who focused least on what was on the plate. Whatever was offered was welcome, the only condition being that it had to be edible. Half cooked, with more salt, no sugar or too spicy nothing really mattered to me; I could polish off the plate with great ease and relish both, the home cooked food and the hostel food with the same gusto, no complaints whatsoever. After getting married and having children, their food choices were of utmost importance to me. Hence, I was happy cooking and eating whatever they favored and never really bothered about my personal preference.

When I perused these Maxims, all of them seemed like a cake walk to me, except for Maxim 7. And, Maxim 8 was the first maxim that I exultantly ticked off, to be followed and made a part of life.

'Be happy to eat in constant divine thought whatever you get, with due regard to honest and pious earnings'.

My upbringing gave me the habit of mumbling a perfunctory 'thank you', offering the first morsel to God before eating, so eating in constant divine thought was done. Also, my husband is typically very upright with his dealings at work. He does not believe in making a single penny on the side. What he works for, he rightfully earns, a law abiding, tax-paying good citizen! So with due regard to 'pious earnings' was also automatically taken care of.

I have happily spent many years in the mission with this myopic, ignorant understanding of this maxim. Master has his own reasons and ways of teaching and opening his abhyasis eyes and mind. I was watching a DVD of Master's Question and answers (Meanderings of Sahaj Marg) and there it was, my foolishness laid bare in front of me, what the maxim meant and encompassed and how aptly I really understood the Maxim came to light.

I was focusing only on the food that went into my digestive system; what was more important was the food I absorbed through my other senses! My eyes look at grossness, rest on it, contemplate over it or do not refute it, acknowledge it, I am hence absorbing grossness, bad food to put it bluntly! And I was seeing, listening, hearing, talking many things not so acceptable, very changeable and causing indigestion to me, my mind –body and soul. When Master said, *'eat in constant divine thought'* He implied that think of HIM while doing anything pertaining to all the senses, not just when you are eating. Food needs to be simple so that it helps you in your meditation and as you progress on your spiritual journey. Sensitivity also grows accordingly. The food ingested also must be subtle or light. We are asked to avoid non- vegetarian food because it is heavy, takes time to digest, plays truant with the senses, causes trouble when meditating and kind of slows down the spiritual progress, as a summation. So does liquor, with liquor the mind is anyway dulled and we are not in our complete senses. How is meditation possible when the senses are not in control? Whatever we eat gets converted and courses through our arteries and veins. Should we not be more considerate and thoughtful about what we are exposing our physical self to? And in the long run it affects our mental well-being too! The heedless eating habit I was practicing was a hindrance to my spiritual progress. I may not be eating wrong, but I was neither adapting the correct attitude towards food!

Master says that as we go on our spiritual path the body tries to get divinized and it needs to be subtler and subtler. The food is not only through our mouth, but from the other sensory organs as well; eyes, touch (skin), ears, nose. Food is not only for our physical nourishment, but also for mental and spiritual progress. Master gives an example in that talk, saying that Babuji (our second Guru) has himself given an example of a man going out, watching a girl dancing on the street. He is fascinated but he is able to (wave it away), walk on. Another man goes ten steps and comes back and says, 'Let me watch it fully'- bandh gaya (trapped). I realized that my understanding of Maxim-8 was that of the second person, the trapped guy!

I do eat simple vegetarian food, but the rest of the intake is a long way from the mark and definitely begging for improvement. A small altercation with anyone in the family and my hackles are raised, my meditation is totally bombarded with thoughts, and I am ashamed to acknowledge that almost all the thoughts are vengeful and disturbing. I am not following correctly the first part of the Maxim itself, so who am I to judge about 'pious earnings' and all. I first need to correct myself and then all falls into place. Every Maxim is intended to help me on the spiritual journey. I have to read in between the lines and try to decipher a more spiritual or innate meaning of these Maxims and follow them correctly, as intended. Else, it is time to take stock and discern where the lacuna is and immediately fill the gap before it becomes a gaping hole. I practically sat smug with a wrong thought for so long..... so many years wasted already!

Even the quantity we eat and the attitude with which we partake of the Prasad makes a difference to our whole being. Prasad eaten with gluttony finds its way out immediately and no change comes in the aspirant who has been eating Prasad for years. That's why Master offers ever so little as Prasad, He wants to let it go in, digest, bring in the change and let the purity run through the person! That little Prasad itself I am unable to digest and allow it to change me. All the gluttony

I showed during Bhandara (our congregations); I realize that I may have to fast for 10 years now to make up for the lost past!

This method and my conscious practice of it keeps teaching me lessons every day and also puts my knowledge to test. I am yet to know, whether my understanding of the system is as my Master meant it to be or have I devised some easy meaning out of it for my own convenience? Even today, I realize that what I know is only the tip of the iceberg. I am still relearning Maxim 8 and putting it to practice the way my Guru would have wished it to be followed.

My success or failure is revealed to me through the comments I receive from my friends and family. I try to self-assess, as realistically as possible, to check how I have fared and how well I have been able to live up to my next maxim, Maxim 9.

MAXIM 9

"Mould your life so as to arouse a feeling of love and piety in others."

This Maxim, according to me, is the summation of all the other Maxims. The day I attain some semblance, even a sliver, that day I will be encouraged to confess that I am nearing the end of this journey, or probably ready to embark on my journey beyond this level. I don't think I can describe or explain this Maxim. I have been contemplating for over a month as to how best and what apt I can write that sagaciously draws the 'perfect' picture of this Maxim in the readers mind. Somehow, words fail me, and I am still at a loss.

To do justice to this Maxim I have to start from the beginning. My prefect's house (*Preceptors are the conduits appointed by our Master from whom aspirants can take 3 introductory sittings and practice guided Meditation*) has a series of photos on the walls of her living room. While meditating on the last day of my three introductory sittings; I was flooded (engulfed) by a bright ray of light for a moment and then suddenly it was totally dark. I saw a figure, an aged man clad in a pristine white garb, I could not figure out what exactly He was wearing. He looked at me, a gaze ever so gentle, loving and His dewy eyes looked straight into me. He extended His hand and lifted me off my seat. I held His hand and He guided me through a flight of stairs, a dark passage way and suddenly there was only light and nothing beyond. I was craning my head and trying to see beyond this light, shielding my eyes and searching for this person when I heard my preceptor say, "That's all". I was snapped out of the reverie and became conscious. I realized that my eyes were also numb and dewy, tears had trickled down and I surreptitiously brushed them away. I was too dazed and my heart was exploding with inexplicable emotions. I kept shaking my head trying to get a grip over myself when my eyes fell on a picture on the wall. This was the same face; wet eyed, gentle, loving face, looking into me and smiling. I asked my prefect who this person was and she replied, "Babuji Maharaj, our second guru."

Those eyes and the love in them made a very deep impression on me. I felt humbled that I was yet to properly embark on this journey and here He was extending His hand, assuring me of His help and presence. I knew I had found my path, a direction in life. For the first time the purpose of this life became clear. I wanted to walk this path and enable myself, to one day leave the same impression on at least one person who crossed my path. His face was an embodiment of love and piety and He made me cry; cry out of gratitude, humility and a profound longing to become like Him took seed.

Only when the ground is prepared, can any seed grow to become a sapling and become a fruit bearing tree. It needs proper care and nurturing. The seed within me also took a lot of beating before it could become a sampling. As days went by I kept falling and getting up time and again. I used to lapse into complacency and something would happen which brought to light a new facet of this path and I realized how little I had accomplished so far.

The training program I attended in Kharagpur was during one of those 'complacent' phases of my abhyaas. The desire to 'become like Him' was missing and 'I know it all' was the mental frame with which I attended this workshop.

I learnt many lessons in Kharagpur but the most poignant of all learning's came on the last day. We had a small activity on the last day which goes like this: The purpose was to go from point A to point B, blindfolded. The first time, we were given a guide, the second time we were asked to accomplish the same journey on our own. The instructions seemed easy and I had a guide for the first round. Psychologically, it did not matter to me that I was blindfolded, my guide was there, right by my side to help me. Thus, I did not hear the instructions. I simply assumed that both the trips were from the same Point A to same point B and I happily allowed myself to be blindfolded. In the first round I bumped into a chair, and a fellow participant, who was acting as my guide, gently steered me and instructed me to change course. I accomplished this trip successfully and was ready to do it on my own. I had cleverly made mental notes, landmarks and all I needed to do was follow them. I did not need a guide anymore.

Even before the race began I started to fumble and crashed into bush. That fall flummoxed me and my direction, position and the mental notes that I had made all flew out of the window. I stood there for a few seconds and tried to calm myself, so that I could reorient, make my way back and restart. It wasn't about winning anymore; even completing the journey was at stake now. I stood there trying to collect my thoughts when I heard my guide's voice gently whispering by my side, "You are going the wrong way, turn around and start walking straight".

That voice was like a Godsend! We were to do this journey on our own, yet the guide was aware of my over confidence or foolishness and was by my side, guiding me the whole time; much like my Master. He knows of my arrogance and stupidity and in His infinite love and wisdom, incessantly kept His eyes on me. I am never out of His sight. I was ashamed of myself. A simple game, the simplest of instructions and I had erred so badly. I shamefacedly continued my walk and covered the distance. When I removed the blind fold I was confronted with yet another blunder. I was the only one standing at that spot. The other participants were already at their destination which was somewhere else! They were all looking at me and I looked back at them, with my guide right behind me, wearing a weak smile. I asked my guide where I had blundered, and she explained that I had started on the same track, fallen and changed course. She had whispered the right direction and yet I had derailed again and ended at this wrong spot. I did not hit any road blocks and was not stumbling either so she simply followed me, on the wrong path! I would realize my folly after removing the blindfold.

I am a Behavioral counselor and Psychotherapist by profession and my key skill is 'listening'. Listening with interest, listening with empathy and listening correctly; these are supposed to be my core skills. This simple game had proved me wrong on all counts. I was so arrogant; I was half deaf. I heard but did not listen to the instructions and neither was I humble enough to take the guidance offered the second time, and reach the right place! Even at that point I immediately set off on my own and reached the wrong spot. How many such mistakes I was making in my day to day events and decision making process, I do not know. How many times was my poor Master coming to my rescue, trying to veer me and redirect me, I do not know either. To top it all, how many times was I not paying heed to Him and He had to face failure or defeat because of me; I do not dare to know!

My Kharagpur trip put me on the lowest rung again. I realized I was still a beginner. I had to work on myself first, follow the Method better, and live this path. Just following this path may take me some distance, but I wanted to walk the whole nine yards, become Him and I realized that I have a long way to go.

My Master's talks keep bringing to the fore my follies and my improvement areas. A recent talk gave another profound insight. We all come with a baggage or a previous birth Karma and until this karmic debt is not repaid completely this cycle of birth keeps repeating. The purpose of this life for me is to bring this balance to 'nil' and see to it that I put an end to this karmic cycle. 'Samsakara' or tendencies are like the river- bed. To get rid of them permanently, stopping the flow of water or drying the river would not do; I had to destroy the bed of the river and annihilate it beyond recognition. I did recognize the grip of these tendencies and I consciously was working towards getting rid of them. This example or comparison of "Samsakara" or tendencies to "river-bed" made by the Master hit me like a ton of bricks. A new insight dawned on me. I was definitely improving and reducing my baggage, stemming the flow of the river, but a small shower (any unpleasantness in life or a challenge unexpected) and this river (of tendencies) was in full spate again...... and I was back to square one! This talk gave me a small peep into my master's role. He works tirelessly for no personal benefit, against so many odds, facing the possibility of failure ever so often and yet remains steadfast in His work, continues to shower me with love and never rebukes me. I was struggling with myself and He was suffering for all of us! Following Him would at best, make me a follower. I aspired for more that day; live with the pain and defeat He lives with, every day and yet continues to smile and shower love, without any expectations.

This Maxim *"Mould your life so as to arouse a feeling of love and piety in others"* describes my guru. He evokes this feeling in every single person who happens to cross His path. For me this Maxim is less of a Maxim and more my epitaph.

I am not yet confident that I have imbibed any maxim perfectly; but, I can humbly acknowledge that I am trying to imbibe them all with utmost sincerity and honesty.

Epilogue: The pivotal 'M'

"The purport is this: the things of the mid-worlds, in which the abhyasi has stagnated, entrap him so thoroughly that it is impossible to proceed further without first getting rid of the network" {CWR-IV, Ch.4}

Since the time I joined the Mission, my whole focus has been on my getting to know, imbibing the three M's; The Method, The Master and The Mission. This has been my earnest endeavor. For me, being a diligent, dedicated abhyasi was earnestly practicing the Method, following the 10 maxims was a way of emulating the Master and hopefully learn to love all like Him and become Him one day. This Mission had offered me a new life and the least I could to do as an expression of my gratitude was contribute in some small way and be one with this wondrous family.

Years down the line; I am still becoming one with the 3 M's. Everyday something happens, and a new revelation reveals itself. Learning everyday has become a natural process, akin to my nature. I still continue to wage a daily war with emotional turmoil. Expectations from the nearest are deeply embedded, complaining continues, I continue to want things my way else get angry, I still get vitriolic with life itself when I face such challenges on a daily basis. Yet, because of meditation, despite these continuing inadequacies, the sense of calm, better acceptance and an overall change in my personality is very visible to my family.

At times, I feel so many years of abhyaas were no good for me. I am still the same, emotional, expecting, and clinging person I was before I joined the Mission. Such rampant thoughts play havoc and I get totally disoriented. I wonder where they all come from, and after so many years of meditation, should they not have worn themselves out? Why do I keep facing the same situations and go through the same upheavals? Such disturbing moments always draw me back to books or videos and my answers come to me.

{CWR IV, Ch3} *"I may as well say that worries and sufferings arise only when there is a conflict between our will and God's will"*.

Gradually, my abhyaas becomes more aware and wholehearted again, seeking and searching within myself and I realize that He, my Master, has always been there, by my side; it is me who turns a deaf ear or a blind eye and gets entrapped in these travails of daily life.

Comparatively, my life has been much more challenging and turbulent after joining meditation than it was prior to my getting acquainted with this path. After starting to meditate, the biggest change that came was the inability to blame others, for the unsavory situations I found myself in. Meditation enabled me to stay calm and accept the challenges, what perturbed me in the past; now I brush away such incidents without batting an eyelid. Probably, that is why as an abhyasi my life has become a continuous roller coaster ride. As a spiritual aspirant and an earnest seeker how could I afford to become complacent?! The second complacency creeps in it implies my moving away from one of the M's! These challenges help me stay connected, aware and alert to His presence and guidance I incessantly receive. If I am not in a thought provoking situation for long I introspect about my association with the 3Ms. Where ever and whenever my will weakens, or my willingness is absent His hands get tied too. My unwilling self becomes His limitation and I slip.

"In other words, unless the intoxication due to wine evaporates, man cannot get rid of the intoxication" {CWR-IV, Ch.4}

Another revelation is my earnestness or love for Him makes me seek work and my rote attitude of 'doing my duty' makes me wait for work to cross my path. Such subtle differences came to light and the inner self mirrors itself in every little thought and action of mine. When changes keep happening every minute how can my life be smooth sailing? Until the pivotal M, does not merge with the other 3 M's, changes will be inevitable, and challenges will surely be more daunting than before.

This hurried life, brimming with potholes and speed-breakers has brought to light another revelation; that at the center of these three M's was another M: Myself. And this M (myself) defined everything, my connection to the Method, Master and Mission and My disassociation of Myself from My Self. Wholehearted abhyaas naturally keeps me driven, fresh on the move and I have the feeling that I can conquer the world, if need be. Volunteering has put me amidst complex people and situations; many things I used to think I will never venture into (not my cup of tea), I have been able to accomplish with ease, giving me an insight into my own strengths and limitations. Loving this path and walking with His hand in mine has taught me that there is nothing me or mine or can do, cannot do work. It is what it is, if it has come in my direction it has come via Him and for a reason. Surrender, acceptance and an inner calm amidst this chaotic noisy outside life seems a possibility only when the pivotal M (myself) is wholeheartedly engrossed in the remaining M's.

This is a life long journey that will end when I go beyond this life is a verity which has finally sunk. And I pray for the moment when the difference between these 4 M's disappears into the oblivion and all become one.

The road to salvation passes through thorns and weeds. I end this book with a humble prayer for my readers, "Break free of these weeds and lead an immortal life"

Thank you

Author Biography

I am a Behavioral Counselor and a Psychotherapist as far as academics is concerned. But inherently I am a seeker, trying to learn something new every day and trying to improve myself with every learning that I receive. Not just live, but be alive and continue to live even after death catches up on me someday. This spirit of enquiry has led me to dabble with many vocations like music, sketching, Painting, cooking and writing (verily a dilettante). I am an instinctive writer and enjoy sharing my experiences and learnings; and this book and the ones that will follow are a compilation of such experiences and learnings.

I have a keen interest in bringing self-awareness amongst children; help them know themselves inside-out, so that they can grow up to be self-assured, content and accomplished adults. Thus, most of the anecdotes pertain to children, parenting, and women. They are real-life experiences or snippets from my own counseling sessions and motherhood times.

Secondly, being a good cook; sharing and learning new healthy and quick recipes seemed to be the next spontaneous choice for me.

My husband and I are both travel freaks. With wheels under our feet, as a family, we have traversed the whole length of India (Kashmir to Kerala); the breadth is still pending. Hence a small travelogue narrating my experiences and hoping the reader will visit these off-beat, yet most charming places in my magnificent country.

The above are my secondary pursuits and passions; my primary goal in life is to emulate and become like my spiritual Guru; merge with Him and realize God through him. My life took a U-turn the day I joined meditation with Shri Ram Chandra Mission. I joined the Mission ten years ago, and from that day onwards, I have only changed for the better; a spiritual birth for me.

The first book is dedicated to my Mission; and the path. The second is my journal and learning from the path. The rest will follow in whichever order my whims lead me toward. I hope you like this book and the ones that will follow, and will be able to connect to at least one genre. If any one person is helped through this series I will consider it a humble accomplishment on my part. All the credit goes to my Guru's blessings and the constant strength I receive from my Mission.

Love and joys always,
Sharanya

Printed in the United States
By Bookmasters